but i cd only whisper

a play by Kristiana Colón

Published by Playdead Press 2012

© Kristiana Colón 2012

Kristiana Colón has asserted her rights under the Copyright, Design and Patents Act, 1988, to be identified as the author of this work.

A CIP catalogue record for this book is available from the British Library.

ISBN 978-0-9574491-1-4

Caution
All rights whatsoever in this play are strictly reserved and application for performance should be sought through the author before rehearsals begin. No performance may be given unless a license has been obtained.

This book is sold subject to the condition that it shall not by way of trade or otherwise, be lent, resold, hired out, or otherwise circulated without the publisher's prior consent in any form of binding or cover other than that in which it is published and without a similar condition including this condition being imposed on the subsequent purchaser.

Playdead Press
www.playdeadpress.com

This play is for soldiers who come home hurting, for their families. This play is for the men whose minds must roil in silence, in the dark. Without the searing honesty and craft of Ntozake Shange, this piece could not exist. Without the love and persistence of Nadia Latif, it would have no voice with which to sing. I also wish to thank Sophie Watson and Tabula Rasa Theatre, Nikki Patin, Marlon Esguerra, Idris Goodwin, Beau O'Reilly, Rob Goodwin, Tiffany Trent, Chuck Smith, and my mother, April Williams.

'but i cd only whisper' includes extracts from 'For Colored Girls Who Have Considered Suicide When The Rainbow Is Enuf' by Ntozake Shange and is reprinted by the permission of Russell & Volkening as agents for the author. Copyright © 1989 Ntozake Shange

Developed with the support of the Lincoln Centre New York

All details correct at time of printing

but i cd only whisper was First performed at the Arcola Theatre Studio 2 on 31 October 2012 presented by Sophie Watson for Tabula Rasa Theatre

Cast
Sian Breckin
Emmanuella Cole
Adetomiwa Edun
Cornell S John
Tunji Kasim
Paul McEwan

Creative
Director: Nadia Latif
Designer: Lorna Ritchie
Choreographer: Imogen Knight
Lighting Designer: Michael Nabarro
Sound Designer: Simon Slater
Sound Assistant: Chris Barlow
Production Manager: Ben Crawford
Stage Manager: Hannah Gore
Casting: Annelie Powell
Projections (editor and co-designer): Wendy Short
Assistant Director: Jane Moriarty
Assistant Producer: Tom Allott
Fight Director: Bret Yount
Dialect Coach: Richard Ryder
Press by Mobius

Kristiana Rae Colón
Playwright
Kristiana is a poet, playwright, actor, educator, & Ensemble member at Teatro Luna. Kristiana has rocked the mic at Chicago's top venues including the Park West, the Aragon, the Metro, Victory Gardens Theater, as well as venues nationwide & in the UK. In Autumn 2012, she opened her solo play *Cry Wolf*. Her play *One Week in Spring* was a finalist in Victory Gardens' 2010 Ignition festival and *but i cd only whisper* won 2nd place in the Theodore Ward Playwriting Competition. She was featured on the 5th season of HBO's Def Poetry Jam. In January 2013, Northwestern University Press will publish her collection of poems *promised instruments*.

Nadia Latif
Director
Directing credits include: *Carrot* (Latitude/Theatre503), *Coalition*, *Slaves*, *Wild Horses* (Theatre503), *The Ballad of Crazy Paola* (Arcola), *In The Heart Of America* (RADA). Associate/assistant credits include: *Decade* (Headlong), *The Great Game* (Tricycle), *The Homecoming* (Almeida), *I Like Mine With A Kiss* (Bush). Nadia was Associate Director of Theatre503 from 2009 to 2011.

Cast
Sian Breckin
Theatre: *Chalet Lines* (Bush Theatre); *24 Hour Plays* (The Old Vic); *The Baron* (The Old Vic/Time Warner Ignite); *The Fool* (Wilton's Music Hall). Television: *Scott & Bailey* (ITV); *DCI Banks: Aftermath* (ITV); *George Gently* (BBC); *Casualty* (BBC); *Heartbeat* (ITV); *The Royal* (ITV); *The Bill* (ITV); *Doctors* (BBC). Film: *Tyrannosaur* (Warp Films/Film Four); *Donkey Punch* (Warp Films/Film Four). Radio: *Shed Town* (BBC Radio 4)

Emmanuella Cole
Theatre: *Roadkill* (Traverse Theatre); *Faith Hope and Charity* (Southwark Playhouse); *Charged: Dancing Bears* (Soho Theatre); *Danton's Death* (National Theatre); *This Wide Night* (Bernie Grant Art Centre); *African Snow* (Trafalgar Studios). TV: *Thorne: Sleepyhead* (SkyOne); *Little Miss Jocelyn, Eastenders & Doctors* (BBC)

Adetomiwa Edun
Adetomiwa made his theatrical debut in *Tiata Delights* at the Almeida. In 2009, he played Romeo in *Romeo and Juliet* at the Globe. Adetomiwa also appeared at the National Theatre in *Macbeth*. His television credits include *The Hour* and *Law and Order*. He has also starred in the popular BBC television series *Merlin* in the role of 'Elyan'. Adetomiwa is a graduate of RADA and Cambridge University.

Tunji Kasim
Theatre: *The Winter's Tale* and *The Grain Store* (RSC); *Duchess of Malfi* (Old Vic); *American Trade, Julius Caesar, Anthony and Cleopatra* and *King Lear* (RSC); *The Brothers Size* (ATC/Young Vic); *The Cracks in my Skin* (Royal

Exchange); *Big White Fog* (Almeida Theatre); *Of Mice and Men* (Oran Mor). Television: *Nearly Famous* (Kudos Film)

Paul McEwan
Theatre: *The Two-Character Play* (Jermyn Street and USA); *Richard II*, *La Lupa* (RSC); *A Midsummer Night's Dream* (Royal Exchange); *Decade* (Theatre503); *The Duel* (Lyric Hammersmith); *Romeo & Juliet* (Hull Truck); *The London Plays* (ORL) and *The Three Musketeers* (Dukes Playhouse). TV: *Eternal Law* (ITV); *Emmerdale* (ITV); *Strictly Confidential* (ITV); *Clocking Off* (BBC); *Dalziel & Pascoe* (BBC); *No Angels* (C4); *Casualty* (BBC); *Holby City* (BBC); *Doctors* (BBC); *Heartbeat* (ITV)

Cornell S John
Theatre: *Waiting for Godot* (WYP); *The Meeting* (Nuffield Theatre); *Slaves* (Theatre503); *The Messiah* (Riverside Studios); *Romeo & Juliet* (Belgrade Coventry); *The Lion King* (Lyceum Theatre); *Porgy and Bess* (Savoy Theatre) *Les Miserable* (Queens Theatre); *The Full Monty* (Prince of Wales Theatre). TV: *Waterloo Road* (BBC); *Inside Men* (BBC); *Top Boy* (Channel 4); *Five Days II* (BBC); *Rastamouse* (BBC). Film: *Dreams of a Life* (Film 4); *Kidulthood / Adulthood* (Revolver/Pathe)

but i cd only whisper

a play by Kristiana Colón

scene

        Early 1970s, inner city. There are three locations in this play: the office, the interrogation room, and the apartment. Each exists in a separate time. The office is the play's present and central universe. The interrogation room scenes are also the present of the play or the very recent past, and may sometimes occur simultaneously with an office scene, or be woven into it. The apartment is the not so distant past.

players

    beau willie brown
african-american male; late 20s

    crystal
african-american female; early 20s

    drummond
african-american male; mid-30s or older

    geneviève
(francophone pronunciation: zhuhn-vyev)
caucasian female; mid-20s to mid-30s

    marshall
caucasian male; late 30s/early 40s or older;

    marvin
african-american male; late 20s to early 30s

a note from the playwright

some scenes are noted as 'prologue' and 'epilogue' instead of having scene numbers. this is to indicate their function with respect to the story, as in a novel, and should not imply that those scenes are optional to produce.

a note on format

Readers will instantly notice the distinct format of the script. It refuses standard spelling, punctuation, and capitalization and instead uses spaces and line breaks. The style originated as an homage to *for colored girls who have considered suicide/when the rainbow is enuf* and its aesthetic, the collection from which this piece's source of inspiration comes. It evolved into an aesthetic and artistic philosophy that challenges the arbitrary nature of grammar and seeks to explore meaning in oral patterns of speech. Actors have found the formatting useful, in that spaces, lines breaks, and the carefully chosen instances of punctuation act as notes on a dramatic sheet of music, and are charged with rich cues for dynamics, volume, tone, and pacing.

act one

PROLOGUE

(beau enters in black. lights rise, dim and blue. beau begins a short choreographed movement interpretation: fighting with crystal, committing his crime, and being arrested. throughout his movement, the sound stops abruptly and starts again, but beau moves through silence, not noticing. he ends empty, remaining still for a few moments.)

ONE

(office lights up to half. drummond enters. he flashes Rorschach cards and records answers as though beau were responding. he does this throughout beau's monologue, occasionally scribbling notes. beau sweats a lot. special on beau.)

beau
she turned eighteen that summer   she was a skinny gal sittin on the crumblin cement stoop of her apartment buildin sippin lime soda outta a sweatin glass bottle
     wrappin her lips round the neck like she wanted it real bad   n she'd sit there waitin for me to get off work   watchin her sisters play hopscotch in the crooked pink chalk boxes they drew on the sidewalk
red n blue barrettes slappin greasy lil shoulders while they jumped   n i'd walk by in my blue uniform dusty round the knees wit my name stitched cross my heart
     hey beau she say real soft   tryna act cool like i'm just the mailman or somethin   n i play that game right back
jus nod   keep walkin

now see i'd jus turn twenty five in april n mama for my
birthday pack all my clothes in a box n my lil tv wit the
broken antenna n lef em all on the porch for when i come
home from crystals house   she said i'm a grown man
n nigga when is you gon get a job   i was real blowed
so i couldn't argue   jus set on the steps n cry a lil bit
fore i picked up the box under one arm   tv under the other
n strut over to marvins place   he the mop man at
woolworths

(marvin enters)

n i know mama says i need to work for once in my life
          so one day marvin come home all sweatin n smellin
like clorox   n i'm on his couch   this nasty
avocado green couch wit cigarette burns all on the cushions
n shit   n i'm watchin i love lucy reruns   smokin a
joint   watchin the fat under fred n ethel's chins jiggle
while they argue   n marvin come in all tired-lookin
in his navy uniform   armpits lookin black for
all the sweat   n i'm sittin there wit no shirt on in my
white boxers n he lookin at me like nigga your triflin ass
need a job but fore he can fix his mouth to start sayin some
shit   i say it's some cold beers in da fridge wit yo name
on em   n i'm bout to roll another joint man
          marvin take off his work shirt n disappear into the
kitchen come back wit two beers lookin like a blessin in his
hot ass apartment   course he ain't got no air n ain't a
single breeze comin through the window screens n the lil
broke down fan jus keep blowin the weed smoke all over   n
he sit down next to me on that ugly green couch
          lucy cryin n ricky yellin at her in mexican n we
both start laughin and slappin our knees
          do it now do it now i say to myself

yeah man so why don't you git me a job at woolworths wit you?
n he stops laughin   look at me real serious like i jus asked him if i could slap his mama upside her head   n start noddin his head real funny like his neck hurt on one side

marvin
yessuh yessuh that's a good idea

(they begin acting out their work day together, sweeping, stacking boxes, etc.)

beau
n by monday i'm wakin up wit marvin   i'm a workin man in my navy blue polyester cleanin up the aisles n stackin boxes in the stock room   n them days i had money in my pocket   crystal would be actin all crazy n cryin all the time so i would cash my check on fridays   put on one of my goin-out suits n head over to jimmys joint   it didn't look like much from the outside but jimmys was always groovin   cats real sharp n smooth-talkin n ladies giggling   asses swayin under their tight skirts n short dresses   johnboy the bartender made the girls drinks real strong n by the end of the night it'd be some fox in my lap wit bright red lipstick n her hair up   runnin fingernails cross the nape of my neck thangs is goin real smooth but marvin say to me one day

marvin
crystal still yo girl?

beau
nigga what is you talkin bout she always belong to me

marvin
aight man but my cousin said he seen her all around town at all hours of the night with some power to the people nigga   some slick cat look like he mixed up with the black panthers

beau
n i think back to me walkin by her n jus noddin n when was the last time i saw her?

marvin
--i know she love you   i was just wonderin is all

beau
friends prolly done filled her head up with jive about me n them girls down at jimmys

marvin
--she prolly just goin to politics meetings   seem like all the fine ladies goin to politics meetings now

beau
n i start getting sick thinkin bout some other nigga smilin down on her big brown ass n her lips whisperin promises into his neck n it feels like somethin done exploded in my brain cuz all i see is white light n crystal burnin in my mind
    i start pullin down boxes n chargin like a mad bull tearin up everything

(lights on marvin fade, he exits)

marvin try to grab hold of me but i can't even see marvin
        all i see is some nigga slippin tween crystals thighs
        mr. pembleton come back there   n i'm
standin over marvin
fists all bloody n i realize what i done   sorry boss
        didn't mean to

        i run outta that store so quick   fast as i can to
marvins to get my tv n box of clothes   now i ain't got no
place to live all cuz that silly bitch can't keep her legs
closed   i'm bout to go to crystals n teach her some
respect n let that bitch know that cuz of her i had no place
to live n needed to move in so her mama would jus have to
learn to deal wit me   n i was walking n come
past theodores appliance store
        n they got bout fifteen big ol color tv sets in the
window   n they all talkin bout the same thing

now i ain't neva been one to get real inspired   specially
not by no tv   but rather than hearing crystals mouth
every morning   seein her mamas draws soakin in the sink
        i got this idea right   i see them tv sets
n i know what i need to do   now i shoulda known it
would be more to it than uniforms n push ups   but food
n a place to stay?   couldn't nothin beat that
not wit me standin wit a box n a black and white
        my blue slacks bloodspeckled   so i say why not
i'll join the army

(crystal enters)

n i'm so happy i forget about beatin crystals ass   i
wanna swing by there n say goodbye   let her know she

can have her black nigga cuz i'm gon be gone at least four
years
maybe more if i do real good   i come by like always n
she sittin outside   her eyes gets real dark like a storm
jus blew in when she see me comin   n i'm whistlin n
laughin thinkin how she'll beg me to stay

crystal
beau. beau please don't walk by here i got something real
important to tell you

beau
i got somethin real important to tell you too   even
though you been actin a fool n givin it up to some
other nigga i ain't even come over here to mess wit you
          i jus wanna say bye

crystal
bye? whatchu mean bye beau i haven't been

beau
n i jus hold my hand up like they do on tv when the man
want his woman to respect his words
no crystal   no excuses   jus listen
          i'm going to the army

TWO

(lights up to full on the office. upon hearing drummond's voice, beau becomes engaged in the present.)

drummond
'nam?

beau
what a bitch

drummond
how so?

beau
it get so you don't know which gooks to shoot   north gooks or south gooks   jungle gooks or village gooks
        boss tell you its ammo in some town   boss tell you them gooks gonna kill the friendly gooks if you don't kill them first   so you shoot   *where's the ammo?*
        screamin gook face against a rock
where's the ammo?   he don't tell you
        he say his wife don't know neither
'cept you don't know what he say cuz he speakin gook
        your buddy get the notion his wife is hiding ammo inside her n he gonna scoop it out   cuz gooks need protecting   n if you don't find ammo in this town might be the next town over   but gooks that don't love america can't be hiding ammo   you saw what the japs did

drummond
were you ordered to do things you found to be immoral?

beau
orders is orders   we all follow orders   what's your orders doc?

drummond
tell me more about crystal

beau
what of her?   got knocked up fore i left   swhat she was cryin bout

drummond
so you're a father?

beau
wudnt so sure   thinkin bobby seale got her legs cocked back

but when i saw them eyes   them was my eyes
          my eyes brand new like they never seen ugly

but i had seen a lotta niggas kilt fore i seen one i give life to
          never did know nothin but knew i wanted to do
that one thing good   make somethin beautiful outta the ugliest nigga that ever lived
naomi was my heart   my reason for livin   only thing keep me alive in that mud watchin crackers get they assholes blowed off   i say i got a fine black woman n beautiful lil girl waitin to meet her papa n i wanna come home a man wit two arms two legs a dick n a chestfulla medals   so i was a soldier   a mean soldier fightin for his baby girl
(drummond prepares to respond, but lights fade to black on the office)

THREE
('interrogation lights.' drummond calmly and deliberately makes his way into the light and takes a seat in the interrogation room.)

drummond

yes sir   yes sir   no sir
               of course   absolutely   of course

this is a matter of competence   comprehension of the crime and ability to participate in a defense
      no but i'm well-aware of the requirement
      yes of course

his understanding of the charges and penalties if convicted
his understanding of courtroom proceedings
recollection of events   facts   motives

well that really depends on the condition of the—   i understand   i see   i see

from the file i've read it's very likely he suffers from post traumatic stress disorder   war neurosis
      well sir i don't know a more layman's way to put it
      no sir   he's a veteran   yes i'm aware of that but regardless of how the army chooses to recognize him the fact remains that he's been to battle   we sometimes find that a traumatic experience may alter one's grasp on reality and ability to reason   it depends on the severity
         well he wouldn't be getting off per se
      he'd be made custody of a psychiatric facility
      no sir he wouldn't be getting off

up to thirty days   how much sooner?   under the law i have up to thirty days   of course i'm qualified   listen—

well <u>that's</u> what i intend to determine

yes i love america what does that have to do with—

but sir—

i see

if i may   why am i the one you called then?
      certainly you don't think that—

gentlemen   gentlemen   please
i will do my very best to get the truth   the truth
      well what the hell else are you looking for
      sir
apologize   no really   that was
inappropriate
i understand   i understand

yes sir   you'll have my report
      when do i meet him?

FOUR

(crystal enters and engages beau, beginning a short movement interpretation of their relationship, swinging violently between abuse and sex. sound ends abruptly with each of them downstage, on opposite sides.)

(special memory lighting on them both. the lines back and forth between crystal and beau are not in the same reality; hers are probably the closest to the truth while beau's are entirely imagined. beau's gesticulation with his exclamations of joy are felt by crystal as various abusive actions, she reacts to his movements as if being beaten, punctuating his words with an interpretation of his violence, i.e. being slapped across the face, arm being twisted behind back, etc)

crystal
army? i'm having a baby beau   it is your baby

beau
hot dog! a father? i'm gon be a daddy? well i'll be damn

crystal
i'm your...naw beau

ain't no other nigga beau please

beau
shoot   what's it gon be you think? bet it'll be a boy
        imagine that   a lil baby boy of my own

crystal
don't! baby please

please!

please i'm pregnant! i'm *–ah!*

beau
thangs gon change baby we git married
       army pay me good so i can buy you thangs
shit   maybe i'll buy me a cadillac

crystal
naw i ain't gonna say dat mess
please beau
please!

beau
buy you a fur coat n a sunday hat!

crystal
i'm...ouch!...i'm

beau
ima buy my boy a horse!   ima take yall to egypt!

crystal
you're hurtin me...naw beau please...i'm your...

(crystal is brought to her knees)

beau
we gon be kings n queens n take our prince to the pyramids!

crystal
(stony)
i'm your bitch   ain't no other nigga been in this
pussy   i'm your bitch beau

beau
that's right baby

you gon be the queen of the nile!

FIVE
(crystal tries to disappear into the floor. tight special on crystal. geneviève appears opposite, perhaps having a cigarette or holding a glass of something strong)

geneviève
boy brown? he's a crazy fuck that's what he is   never was quite right n killin gooks didn't make it any better

    met him the year before he left   sure we had good times   jimmys   see my sister marie is much older n me   when she was young n i was just a girl she'd go to nigger clubs n watch em play their horn   find the handsomest boy there n go home with him n take him to the pearly gates n back

    she'd come home late real quiet not to wake papa who'd kill her dead if he knew she was beddin down with black boys   she'd put her robe on n sit on the edge of my bed while she put curlers in her hair n say   you know the piano music ms mcdougal teaches us? well it's nothin like that

    it's somethin the negroes got that other folks don't that make em so holy when they get a hold of some music

    i mean they play to your soul geneviève they get way down in you n open somethin up

    first i'm just sittin there tappin my foot   then it's a river of sound coursin hot through me   it's like that in the bed too geneviève
When a Negro makes love to you, it's a jazz song, a whole brass combo in your body.

drummond
did you have many affairs while you and crystal were together?

(beau is restless)

geneviève
course a lot of things changed since marie's day

(crystal is slowly, painfully, pulled up to her feet)

beau
i'm jus a reglar man doc

geneviève
with negro rights n all that   not scared one bit to meet your eyes

drummond
regular men aren't faithful?

geneviève
started goin to jimmys cuz they got the best friday night music

beau
jus cuz i'se silly nuff to fall for that dumb gal don't mean i wudnt gon have my fun

(beau ends up, as if by coincidence, in the memory of geneviève where she is introducing herself.)

geneviève
geneviève

beau
that's a lil too fancy for me

geneviève
it's french   papa was a regular yankee but wanted my
sister n me to have classy names
you can call me genie

drummond
i see

geneviève
rum n coke will do me just fine

drummond
did crystal know about the affairs?

geneviève
the heat in here is making me dizzy   let's go to my
place n i'll make you some coffee

(quick black)

SIX

(drummond's voice brings beau back into the present moment with him. crystal still exists in the memory downstage. during the following lines, leading up to her own, she becomes stoic, faces the 'authorities'.)

drummond
so you were happy to hear she was pregnant?

beau
course i was

crystal
beau willie brown

drummond
you had just assaulted your best friend   you thought she had been sleeping with another man

(crystal addresses 'the authorities,' not physically present.)

crystal
april 13th 1942

beau
i was a lil fired up

crystal
one hunred n seventy some pounds

drummond
did you and crystal argue?

crystal
no i do <u>not</u> want to press charges

beau
crystal been my girl since fore she had titties

crystal
don't but maam me

beau
course we fuss every now n again

crystal
he's the father of my baby

beau
sometime she git a lil too fresh

crystal
n i don't intend to send another black man to jail

drummond
...and you would beat her?

(quick fade on crystal, she exits)

SEVEN

(several years later)

(lights up on geneviève and beau downstage. they have just finished making love.)

geneviève
what's her name again?

beau
crystal

geneviève
you love her?

beau
don't know

geneviève
      you love me?

(beau looks)

geneviève
let's go somewhere beau   anywhere in the world

beau
i ain't never been nowhere before   'cept---
      that don't really count

geneviève
pick anywhere   let's go together

beau
when i went i said   yall gon teach me to run one a
these thangs?   they laughed

geneviève
i can make a little money   we'll go somewhere n get
married

beau
we was a million miles in the air a city of clouds   i
looked out the window the whole time   thought i
might see a angel or god or somethin   flyin by
real quiet cuz we not supposed to see em jus flyin around
like that   so i look out the window tryin not to blink
     when i got outta that thang i said damn i gotta
learn how to do that   yall gon teach me to run one a
these thangs?   they laughed

geneviève
how about canada?   they wouldnt be so mean to us
there   or mexico   we could go to the theater
or out dancing   we could go anywhere we wanted
     nobody would even look except to say what a
lucky woman with a big handsome boy like that

(beau looks, incredulous)

geneviève
let's go   i can make a little money   just give
me some time   you love me   let's get out of town beau
     forget crystal and the baby and let's just—

beau
stop it genie

geneviève
we'll send them money if you want   but you deserve
to be happy beau   we'll just—

beau
dammit genie would you give it a rest   what the hell i
look like in canada with a white woman   lost your
damn mind   with a white woman sendin my daughter
white woman's money
lost your goddamn mind

(beau stands, straightens himself and exits. geneviève looks after him, a little too drunk to be as wounded as she'd like to be)

EIGHT

('interrogation room' lights up on crystal, opposite of where geneviève and beau were.)

crystal
yeah. i'm here. again.
i don't know what's left

strange idnt it
everytime i see badges it's through blacked n swollen eyes
think i'll write a poem bout that one day
yall think i'm stupid.   it's my fault   i coulda stopped this.

(briefly loses then regains composure)

crystal
don't!   i don't need your—
what am i sposed to do?   he was twenty
         i was thirteen
boy called blackjack lived in my building beau would come to buy herb from

(special on beau, at age twenty. clean. sober. he notices her. tries to get her attention. she resists his flirtation and tries to stay focused on the 'authorities')

beau was so slick then i remember   n sweet
don't know how he got bread those days but he was always so sharp
think he was doin somethin straight back then   only
street thing he did i think was smoke herb

(crystal is seduced into the memory)

anyhow my cousin had braided my hair n put shine on my lips   she was seventeen n thought i was some kind of babydoll

(beau crowds her space in a way that straddles the line between sexy and creepy. even as she interacts with beau, crystal narrates the events to the 'authorities,' turning to address them as beau caresses her face, etc as if he is not there)

crystal
i was on the first stairwell up n spose beau had just come from blackjacks pad leavin on his way to do whatever cool cats like him did them days

beau
slow down sweetheart

crystal
he said

beau
where you off to so fast?

crystal
i was runnin   don't recall why
he stepped in front of me   smellin like a man n he was so much taller   i was still outta breath
    chest heavin n him bein close to me   lookin at me like that made me start tremblin

beau
you scared?

crystal
i jus shook my head n stepped back up ginst the wall
        so cool on my bare shoulders

beau
you're very pretty miss lady

crystal
he pulled my chin up so i could see his eyes   cupped
his big hand round my cheek
i closed my eyes n leaned a little into his hand

(they kiss)

crystal
i could feel his private parts gettin hard
pokin right below my belly button   my heart beatin
faster than war drums   n started to feel wet in my jeans so
i tore myself from tween him n the wall   ran up to
my place   slammed the door n went straight to the
toilet cuz i thought i'd peed myself

course i hadn't   i was just excited n too young to
know what that meant

(beau lusts)

but soon after he showed me

(beau fades back into the office)

so what am i sposed to do?
everything i know bout bein a woman i learned under him
n i hear you sneer

you n the neighbors on the eighth floor
kinda woman is she?
only kind i ever learned n a strong one too

(fade on crystal. lights on the office.)

NINE

drummond
you were violently abusive mr. brown

(beau waves him off. drummond hands him a folder filled with crystal's hospital reports and photos of her injuries.)

drummond
crystal tells you she's pregnant with your son
        did you try to cut off her breast with a broken bottle?

beau
i told the cops a million times   she fell on that bottle

drummond
you knocked her down?

beau
grown folks disagree doc   you ever disagree wit yo woman? you got a woman? you some kinda sissy?

drummond
i've never hit a woman   i've never hurt a woman

beau
you always hurt the ones you love   ain't you never heard that sayin doc?

drummond
love does come with disappointments   mistakes
        but not fractured ribs

beau
you prolly only know white folks sayins

drummond
it got worse after you got back from vietnam

beau
(sings) …the ones you shouldn't hurt at all   you like the mills brothers doc?

drummond
barbershop   the steamboat four?

beau
now they were slick! wasn't they slick!
                (sings) if i broke your heart last night it's because i love you most of all

drummond
i got that paper doll record   that's a good record

beau
yes indeed doc!   boy they were slick!   i shoulda been a singer doc   wavy black hair look like mink n a little bitty mustache   du wop n finger snap on the dean martin show   i shoulda sang

drummond
instead of a soldier?

beau
clean white suit n a black bowtie   black pocket square   black wingtip   wasn't they clean doc

drummond
you shoulda been clean

beau
i shoulda been clean   that's right

drummond
did you feel clean when you got home from 'nam?

beau
some ugly don't clean up with a nice suit

drummond
that must have been difficult beau   coming
back home to your family   feeling ugly

beau
(sings) you always break…

drummond
you were violent with your family   your son
was injured

beau
i wudnt never hurt kwame beau jr   or my pretty
naomi   thems my best thangs

drummond
tell me more about 'nam

(beau makes himself invisible)

-

drummond
what do you remember about vietnam?

do you remember?
-
(beau seethes)

beau
think i'm crazy?might be　　　　tellin your woman to shut
the hell up with all that bitchin while i'm tryna drink my
mornin coffee　　n teachin her not to do it again　　maybe
that's crazy
don't rightly know myself　　　　never did much school n
don't know what your high n mighty school say crazy is

but i know a few thangs　　　　one of em is any charlie
laughin n hootin watchin womens skin boil off they face
cuz his cracker buddies is napalmin a village is helluva lot
crazier n me i know that
man ain't built to stay sane in that country
even without the smilin white boys gettin hard ons from
ugly death
the mud
the mud whispers
n hisses
n makes fun of ya when ya can't run fast enough
cuz it's suckin on your boots already heavy wit your swole
feet
n it steams with shit and blood and meltin skin
like the goddamn guts of hell

(marshall enters 'interrogation room')

TEN

('interrogation room' lights on marshall)

marshall
sergeant major reginald marshall
united states army

beau
i come home from that n crystal cryin bout some damn diapers

marshall
he was in my battalion

beau
gettin knocked up again

marshall
had a knack for killing but didn't seem to like it much

beau
i wanna go back to school n that silly bitch went n got pregnant

marshall
was dumb as dogshit and a little strange it seemed talked about his daughter a lot guess she'd be about two when i met him he got sent home not too long after

drummond
you blame her for becoming pregnant?

marshall
now look   i know why you boys called me here

beau
slut if i ever knew one

marshall
(amused) you think i can prove or not prove – disprove as you boys might say – whether or not he's crazy

drummond
mr. brown

beau
come up on my neck breathin hard smellin like coconut n wet cat

marshall
if <u>viet-NAM</u> made him crazy

drummond
mr. brown?   who did?

marshall
fine <u>upstanding</u> gentlemen like you   you've seen a lot i imagine   how long you been here son?

beau
can hear she been cryin even fore i turn around
        but she reach around n grab me

marshall
bet you seen some whoppers in your time huh?
bank robberies   <u>stabbings</u>   child <u>ab</u>-duction

drummond
who?

beau
just rained n mosquitoes still eatin me alive after eighteen months

marshall
suicides. <u>homicides.</u> arson.

beau
(laughing bizarrely, detachedly) ha! i was drunker n luke at the last supper!

marshall
i have served my country for twenty two years

(beau is becoming increasingly more agitated)

beau
pissin by the trash out back

marshall
i don't have sob stories about what i <u>seen</u> okay?
there's no violin player stationed by my pillow at night

beau
private isaacs n private brooks   always loved a laugh at a darkies expense

drummond
i think it's time we take a break mr. brown

beau
sent her over i guess   reached around n grabbed me
(beau begins pacing furiously, grabbing his head, pulling at his collar)

marshall
so do i think private... excuse me... mister beau willie brown is mentally unsound
         probably so

beau
can't be more than seventeen   n then she—

they standing by the street   whistlin n hootin

(drummond becomes seriously concerned, stands and approaches beau)

beau	**marshall**
cheerin like it's the goddamn homecoming football game	do i think war did it to him?
(drummond places a hand on beau's shoulder, beau reacts much as he did with marvin, but drummond grabs his hand before he can strike and wrestles him to a sitting position on the floor)	**marshall** sir i do believe that boy was as loony as daffy duck the day his mammy spat him out

(lights down, special on beau remains, then fade to black. marshall exits)

ELEVEN

(special on marvin, opposite of where marshall was. marvin sits in silence for several moments, but he is animatedly, though somberly, wrestling with a thought. he starts as if he is going to speak several times before he does. marvin may sometimes laugh at inappropriate moments because he is uncomfortable)

marvin
what you say he done now?

-

hm
i – you gotta understand

people been talkin a whole lot i know
and i'll tell you – i know how this may sound but – i'm kinda glad

not that—
no that'd be awful but—
just seems like more fuss than usual over niggers killin each other

and i mean no disrespect   but we are all men here
           and you know well as i do officer...

(measured, struggling to articulate)

yall got any ideas where beau and me came up?
sure you do   yall are up there all the time

death come round like the ICE.   CREAM.   TRUCK.
dig?
so all this talkin and storytellin
i don't know   i don't know what
i suppose crystal had something to do with why

and don't get me wrong now
i ain't saying it's <u>alright</u>
but
i known beau since....

      we were fools!

i ain't gonna sit here and judge no siree
cuz it coulda been me   you know that it
coulda been <u>any</u> of us
do you understand that?
so beau come back from 'nam with empty eyes and hands
like stone
but
the war started long before he got on that plane officer
it coulda been me   it coulda been <u>anybody</u>
all this talkin... not on our block
no white coats askin us how we feel then
so if me and the rest of the boys find this kinda funny
      you'll have to excuse us i mean
<u>ain't no badge ever stop to ask us our story before</u>
dig?

pigs got blackjack
beau mama kill herself

so when i see white folk on tv sittin back on some head
doctor's brown leather couch...

37

      it coulda been <u>any</u> of us officer
where beau and me from... it's enough wonderin if you'll
walk again after pigs crack your head open
if the price of bread and diapers go up this week   if
woolworth gonna clean up its image so that black boys
can't even mop

so yeah it coulda been me
beau ain't particularly more crazy than the rest of us
just nothin set us off yet

for a black man officer   wounds are of the flesh   dig?

think too long about what's deeper than that
we'd all be as loopy as the mad hatter

(lights down on marvin, he exits)

TWELVE

(lights on the office)

drummond
beau willie brown

(helps beau to his feet and brusquely sits him back in his chair)

Let me explain a few things to you.
I am a grown man and this is my office. I will not be threatened in my office.
You do not want the men outside this office to know that you have threatened me.

Can you hear me mr. brown?

I want us to be perfectly clear.
There is a lot of discussion about you, mr. brown.
You're a regular celebrity.
I go home at night and my neighbors <u>ask</u> me about you.
They want to know if the lunatic nigger is going to get locked up or not.
They know I got something to do with that.
So every evening, I tip my hat and say to some powdery gossip
"Ma'am, so kind of you to ask after mr. brown, but confidentiality prohibits my discussion of how he's faring."

Do you understand me?

Do you want to know why?

Everyone wants to know if when we come out of this room, if I will say you're a monster, a bad seed. They want to know mr. brown. If I will say you are just misunderstood. Temporarily insane.

And you know, I still don't know what I'm going to say.

Look at me. I'm a black man.
I know what a black man can do.
I—

Do you hear me?

Let's not make this much more difficult.
When I come out of this room, no matter what I say, people will be angry.
I come out of here saying you couldn't help it, didn't know, just a sad, crazy – need rehabilitation, hospital not a prison— I say that, how my white neighbors going to look at me while they trim their rose bushes? The prosecutor and the detectives? My supervisor and the other doctors? And I say you're a guilty man? You knew what you were doing, send him to the gas, to the electric chair – make him pay, he's a danger to society— then what? How does my pastor look at me when I pass my tithe down the aisle? The deacons and the choir…how do I look black people in the eye, and they know I sentenced one of us to death.

Are you listening to me mr. brown? Do you understand?

beau
dr. drummond   she cudnta been more n seventeen

drummond
mr. brown. okay.

beau
you ever been anywhere doc?

drummond
i'm sorry?

beau
like on a airplane?

drummond
I flew to Boston once.

beau
huh.   only planes i ever been on   well wudnt no peanuts you know   no bubble water or pillow

drummond
Do you want to tell me what happened?

-

She was only seventeen.

She was crying.

Who was she?

Why was she crying?

(beau's mind panicks, but his body is paralyzed)

beau
i gotta get outta here doc   crystal'll never shut up if i don't get back with some milk

drummond
mr. brown

Do you understand what has happened?

beau
naomi prolly cryin bout her daddy been gon too long
    swhat crystal always say she do

drummond
    Jesus

beau
how long we been in here now

drummond
Do you need a break?

beau
(dazed and nearly catatonic)

we been in here a thousand hours doc   i gotta go
    i gotta get back

doc?   how much longer we gon be you think doc?
    can i least go get some milk for the babies?

i really gotta get a move on doc...

we   been   in   here   a   milllllion daysssss

(lights on office fade to black but specials remain on beau and drummond's faces, then fade slow to black.)

- end of act one -

act two

ONE

(marvin and crystal in opposite interrogation rooms)

crystal
he would feed me apples

marvin
his mama had burn scars   made her crazy

crystal
summer so hot out on the stoop   hotter in the buildin though

marvin
she had been pretty before beau   before the burns
    so beau stayed with us a lot

crystal
i don't know how the girls jump rope all day when it's so hot   i just sit on the stoop wishin somebody come talk to me   makin up stories in my head   makin up friends

marvin
my mama made sure he ate   his mama cuss at him n say ugly things   his mama all day tryna forget she was pretty   get so beau don't eat you dig?
my mama make sure we both eat

crystal
beau go up to my mama's kitchen n cut up apples   i stay out sittin on the stoop cuz i gotta watch my sisters
      i go inside n they get snatched mama kill me
      so i stay out while beau cut up apples n bring em down in a cold bowl   sit next to me on the stoop n listen while i dream n talk n remember things
      interrupt me with a apple slice   smile while i chew
      beau act like the only thing more important than whatever words i'm spinnin is that i eat cold apples on a hot day that he feed me

marvin
beau is always the biggest thing in the room   he like a magic trick at a dinner party

crystal
i talk n folk don't understand   folk say i should come down a peg   i talk n beau don't understand
well beau used to not understanding   beau just like the colors

marvin
well yeah   sometimes the trick is cuttin someone in two

crystal
when someone love you like that   n one morning it just goes away   you wanna break yourself apart tryna figure out why

marvin
but at least you're in the room

crystal
what thing in you made them change they mind about loving you so much

marvin
beau got this way of makin you your biggest self
    or makin you invisible

crystal
so you rip your middle open to see what ugly thing you are
    what made him walk away

marvin
but really he's just glass

crystal
but you never find it

marvin
mirror   showin you what you are

crystal
it's nothing there

(marvin and crystal cross to leave the interrogation rooms. they collide with a memory outside of the apartment.)

crystal
oh   beau ain't here now

marvin
he be here soon   why don't you come with us?

crystal
come where?

marvin
my uncle drivin us down to kentucky

crystal
what for?

marvin
get out the city some   got folks down there   music

crystal
my mama never let me leave my sisters for the weekend

marvin
beau ain't ask you to come?   beau shoulda asked you to come

crystal
beau likes secrets

marvin
it be nice to hear you laugh

crystal
it be nice to laugh

marvin
your sisters big enough to watch themselves one weekend

crystal
mama won't think so

marvin
you're almost a woman

crystal
beau said he'll meet you here?

marvin
any minute

crystal
good   i'll stay out on the stoop n give him a kiss fore yall go

marvin
you ever been out the city?   catch lightning bugs?

crystal
it's lightning bugs in the city too

marvin
you should come out the city some   fresh air do you some good

crystal
fresh air do all us good   specially beau

TWO

(lights up to dim on the office, special on beau)

beau
i was always in pieces   long as i could remember
put together some sometimes   other times all every
which way n can't find em all and

well
i mean
you ever seen a piece of crystal? a real one?
take pieces of light   all kinds
    take a piece from the sun   from the street
light   take a piece from the match i use to light a square
    yeah it take some from the liquor store sign n even
from the pigs siren
crystal take all kindsa pieces of light   the pretty n the
ugly kinds   take it inside n put out a rainbow

you ever seen a real piece of crystal?

take in all them pieces of light n put out somethin…

(short burst of laughter)

first time i seent one i sho nuff cried   who makes
somethin like that?
somethin that can turn a whole lotta mess into the most
beautiful thang you ever saw

so i seen my piece
n i say "what they call you pretty lady?"

boy i tell you   you coulda knocked me cold right there
when she said it

n i thought   maybe she could do that to my pieces?
you think beau?
she could take in all the niggers n coons n hereboys you
been called   all the ugly n the bigtoothed laugh?
think she like the real thang n can take in all your pieces n
put em together n make somethin beautiful?
somethin even whitefolks would stop n look at?
somethin so beautiful crackers would be ashamed of their
guns n drop em in the vines to be swallowed by the mud

you ever seen a piece of real crystal?

man and she could!
funny thing when somebody love you like you was they
own self

all the pieces get together n act right n then sometimes...

man that's all right
that's all right

but
guess she wasn't no real thang
cuz   after awhile   they jus fall back
no real piece of crystal would let light fall back into the
street lamp n be ugly again

n she jus keep lovin harder n harder pretendin she not a
fake n pieces keep fallin back n man

ain't nobody ever loved you so hard you felt like a monster?
see yourself in a mirror n don't even look like you
        some other thing
dark n tangled up
like the little girls faces in the village by the rice fields

try to get her to stop doin all that lovin so your face can come back n you can try to get the pieces back in order
        try to make her stop

till she just layin there   n won't move
actin like she can't get up

but summer times man!   summer!
summer flip n i think she's the real thang again n so i try to put my piece of crystal back together
i thought it was fake n broke it into bits but summer flip n her thighs get brown n her back shiiiiiiiine

we drink sugar   can't get enough
snow cones n kool aid n popsicles n more snow cones again till our lips are numb n all the colors of the rainbow n we can't even feel the kissin

it's like that in the summer time

i braid her hair…..ha!
she look like the scarecrow when i do it   but pretty still
n lovin me like she's the real thing

that's what it is doc
can't tell it no bettern'at
(fade to black on beau)

THREE

(geneviève, downstage special)

geneviève
now i want you boys to listen n listen to me good
who's running this outfit anyway? because you got your
facts all mixed up

boy brown could never do something like that

you need to be asking that gal the right questions
        she's caused him so much trouble over the years
calling the cops with every breed of wild lie you could think
of

i never could figure out why he wouldn't just leave her

then of course she started having the babies so naturally he
was gonna stick around

boy brown is a good man   but you know afro-
americans don't have a lot of chances here   and i
don't know why you boys insist on making extra trouble
for the good hardworking ones

he said to me once
it was the cutest thing really
he said
genie you think your daddy would stop calling us niggers if
i could take you to the top of the eiffel tower?
i mean fly you straight to paris where they would say your
name better than even he could
if i saved a little from the taxi cab each night

one day i could buy a airplane n fly you to france genie
n then we danced slow in the parlor to no music at all and
he gave me a bubble bath.........
 i tell you   that black bitch just didn't know how to
treat a man like that
if you ask me she's the one that did it   or maybe
one of her pimps   bet you boys didn't know that did
you   who's running this outfit anyway?
            because you don't have the facts
            boy brown couldn't do that   n she is a no-good
tramp   walked all over that good boy's heart and never
would let him go

you ever suppose this whole thing was just her way of
taking him away from me for good? she's sneaky like that
you know

check it out boys
because you don't have all the facts

FOUR

(beau is much more relaxed now. he sits in his proper chair, somewhat numbly – facing drummond. drummond now understands that there may be a specific event in vietnam that triggered beau's descent into psychosis and is trying to gently bring it to light)

drummond
would you like some water?

beau
what else you got in here?

drummond
just water   would you like some?

beau
surely would

(drummond pulls a plastic cup from one of his desk drawers and pours from a pitcher set on a small table set upstage. he hands the cup to beau, who gulps it down in a breath and extends the cup back out to drummond who unflinchingly refills it and returns it to beau as he resumes his seat)

drummond
mr. brown   do you know why you are here?

beau
you tryna get inside my head

drummond
i'm trying to understand you better yes   do you know why that is?

beau
white folk pay you to

drummond
yes i am a psychologist   normally i work in an office with other doctors   mostly caucasian   we have a practice   we   usually see married couples who are having problems   lonely housewives trying to figure out their purpose

(beau is drifting)

wealthy adolescents angry at their parents   young businessmen bragging of sexual conquests—

beau?

beau
you let white folk tell you they bidness like that?
          dangerous thing doc

drummond
i'm sorry?

beau
someone told me once don't let no white man tell you his secrets cuz later he'll hate you for knowin

drummond
do you know why i'm talking to you today?

beau
tryna get in my head   you asked me that

(beau stiffens as drummond responds)

drummond
while my practice is generally limited to the more marshmallow mundane   i happen to specialize in criminal psychology   of course i never got to practice because who am i to call a white man crazy...

but for some reason i got a call to —

beau you are being charged with a crime

beau
i tell you brother once they git you they always got you ain't that the truth

(laughingly)

what i do now?   too dumb to rob a bank
      too broke to buy a gun   get high every now n then but so do ray charles n he richer than your boss
          ha!

i ain't yo man doc! keep ooooooooooon lookin!

anyhow if they was tryna get me wouldn't be talkin to you all night n day i know!
      they have me in a cell with fifteen sweatin niggas waitin to use the telephone

(claps his hands delightedly)

drummond
mr.—

beau
you know i like you doc

beau
you got a good sense a humor

(drummond takes notes furiously, stands to pour himself a cup of water)

drummond
would you like some more water?

(beau cheerfully extends his cup to drummond who refills it. marshall enters.)

beau
let me guess   i blew up a buildin!   i killed twenty men in one night!   i raided homes n stole they bread n fine china!   i did doc   i really did!

drummond
beau let's talk about –

beau
slap the cuffs on me and lock me away   by god i was a soldier!

(beau grows suddenly but deeply indignant, however proceeds evenly)

lotsa crimes i could be charged with doc
me n mr. co-mmand-o in chief hisself both
so whatchu wanna say i did?

(interrogation lights up on marshall)

marshall
i say he's lucky

drummond
yes beau   let's talk more about vietnam

beau
was a war   i fought in it   killed lotsa gooks

drummond
you would say you were a good soldier?

marshall
i'm from mississippi   summers hot there

beau
ain't no such a thang   there's live soldiers n dead ones i had no mind to be dyin <u>there</u>

marshall
sometimes boys—i'm sure you big city boys get this too—
they get just like mad dogs
all stir crazy from the heat

drummond
did you stay in touch with your friends here?

marshall
my grandpa still had his farm   he was a military man too

beau
naw

marshall
fought next to general lee himself!

beau
awwww

marshall
when i was a boy he found a colored man in his barn one night

beau
genie

marshall
stealing milk from a cow he said

beau
she would send me pictures!

marshall
squirtin it into something ridiculous

beau
never intended to show none a the boys

marshall
a tea cup   or a canteen   something strange

beau
theyda shot me in my sleep sho nuff

marshall
said it was the hottest august since 1879

beau
crystal sent me poems

marshall
and this negro had gone stark raving mad

beau
i read the shorter ones

marshall
bursting into shrill laughter

beau
some went on for pages

marshall
something about the cow being named mary lou and his grandpa having birthed her

beau
but genie's pictures!

marshall
taking what's owed him

beau
legs a mile of white silk

marshall
poor fella probably didn't know his own name

beau
cream in my coffee   i tell you

marshall
and grandpa was mostly an even tempered man   but in his old age

drummond
did any of the other men ever find out you were seeing a white woman?

marshall
wasn't much he could do himself   he was just barely living   but the menfolk were restless

the heat

beau
it's how i became so popular

marshall
that's why i say he's lucky   not many crazy colored stay living long as he has   specially with what you boys are thinking he's done

(quick fade on marshall.)

drummond
they gave you a hard time about it?

beau
private isaacs n private brooks

drummond
you mentioned them before   they played a prank on you?

beau
like i said   i ain't do much schoolin so correct me if i'm wrong doc
but ain't pranks supposed to be funny?

drummond
are you ready to talk about it now?

(snap black on office)

FIVE

(snap lights on interrogation room)

marvin
i watch em   old men with white stubble wine glistenin
in their whiskers
writhin their rattlin bones under street lamps

it's august and the sun gone down and they sweatin in
second hand synthetics
gnawin they lips like they still play harmonica
swattin phantom flies and yankin at they collars

i see em   or it's rainin and they tilted gainst the
scratched brick   under the yellow awning of a
liquor store kickin at empty cans poking outta brown bags

they mumbling bout shirley
              smackin they hollow chest
                      hollerin like the smiling adlib of a
     james brown ballad

i watch em   right around time beau was born they
started puttin japanese in camps   beau was born
inta the worse war this whole planet ever seen   it was like
he knew it   like he saw it   like he carry all them
bodies in his belly   he been fightin since he got here
     maybe was born to fight   maybe swhy he fit
in so right with the army   we grow up watchin the
men who came home   some of em still smiling
bout french girls and all the cities they seen
       some of em sullen n won't come out the house

           but it's a whole bunch   a whole legion
          jus walkin the streets
laughin n screamin   whisperin blues songs hoarse from
all the whiskey

n i watch em   i watch em every day   they tapdancin on
the sidewalk in brown leather loafers over the polka dots of
flattened chewing gum

i see em   n i wonder where they daughter at
     why someone don't bring em a jacket or wipe the
spittle from his chin   why someone don't ease
the bottle of jack from his knuckles
i see em in the early spring gaspin up fog   n i wanna
invite em over for easter dinner   make em feel like
a man   ask him to say grace n pass the greens

i watch em noddin on park benches in the heat of the day
with ketchup stains all down his poked out belly
     jumpin up like a soldier every time a squirrel
skitter by

scowl like he don't remember why kids exist   ice cream
    who ever heard of such a silly wasteful thing
    he scowl like don't remember why kids exist
     why things get born   why people dare to make
more people in a world wit bombs that can blow up whole
cities

beau come back   n i see it in him too   thought
he like to kill himself druggin up so he don't remember
but this   i never expected this   not in a million
years
(lights fade on marvin)

SIX

(marshall and beau sit in the vietnam hooch. "sing a simple song" by sly and the family stone plays on a small radio whose reception crackles in and out.)

beau
--n i told her she was fine   but her mama make better cornbread

marshall
you really never stop flimflammin all colors of a tale

beau
i only speak the truth sarge   i like a woman with lines in her smile

marshall
no siree   i like them young and trusting
        whole

beau
when i get back i'm goin straight to jimmys
get some real whiskey n a fine woman

marshall
aw this mountain goat bathtub piss don't stack up to your city boy whiskey?

beau
you look like a man that knows his whiskey

marshall
whiskey war and women   that's all i know

beau
i heard that!

marshall
cheers

beau
cheers!

('jumpin jack flash' by the rolling stones plays on radio.)

beau
(takes a long swing)
wish i could hear these tunes while we out in the mud sarge
    seem like to move faster if we had some driving
tunes out there

marshall
rock n roll is war music

beau
i wouldn't figure you for a rock n roll type

marshall
i ain't   can't have music in the battle private
    breath gotta be the music
bullets gotta be the drum

beau
not even the beatles?   think i'd kill more a them gooks if
ringo had a kit set up in them vines   mud flyin off his
sticks   keep the rhythm

marshall
boots gotta be the rhythm beau   gotta hear the blood   can't hear blood over rock drums

beau
what song would you have sarge? if you had a song to play the battle
what song you pick?

marshall
ahh well   guess it'd have to be   oh i don't know
i said there can't be no music

beau
i know what you said   i know it can't be   you know
it can't   but just imagine   can't you imagine
sarge   if it was a song blastin down from the sky
       blastin down through the trees   what
song would you want to hear out there?
              a gospel song?

marshall
no   no beau   not a gospel song

beau
play pretend   imagine   don't you never imagine?

marshall
it's enough to think about what is without trying to figure some of what ain't

beau
just imagine sarge   would it be a jazz song? you dig jazz?

marshall
no private   no jazz
guess it would have to be riders in the sky
     riders in the sky   vaughn monroe

beau
ahhh country   shoulda figured you for a country man
     southern man

marshall
i'm a country man i suppose   a southerner that's sure

beau
uh huh

marshall
an american man beau   what are you?

beau
a war man   nothing but a war man sarge

marshall
that's sure   what were you before here?

beau
nothin   i wasn't nothin

marshall
you and me both private   you and me both
i wasn't nothin before war

beau
but we here now sarge! we here now!

marshall
we are here   and ain't it a gas

beau
say cheers!

marshall
cheers!

(lights fade up on office. beau stumbles out of the hooch and into the office. geneviève narrates a letter she wrote to beau while he was in vietnam. beau argues with isaacs and brooks, not present. marshall addresses 'the authorities' from the interrogation room)

drummond
tell me more about the prank   private isaacs and private brooks

geneviève
my darling beau

beau
fellas   fellas please   aww it ain't nothing   jus a lil note from home

geneviève
i miss you more than words

marshall
I am aware that he received some correspondence from a White woman

geneviève
my body aches for your big   brown   hands

beau
come on now boys now stop that   it's jus a lil letter
that's all

marshall
of the sexual nature.

geneviève
searchin every inch of me

beau
please   naw now brooks   naw it ain't like
that   come on now

marshall
I understand there may have on occasion   been
some <u>photographs</u> included

beau
give that—   isaacs   yall don't see me snatchin
at your personal affairs

gimme—!

marshall
<u>nude</u> photographs.

geneviève
i absolutely burn with thoughts of us

marshall
he was a fine soldier   a hero some might say
        but he had no right

geneviève
please think of me

beau
she—   naw fellas she—   it ain't like that i swear

geneviève
after lights out   send some kissin thoughts my way

beau
please yall   ya gotta understand   please

marshall
and I know I'm not the only one that thinks that way.

geneviève
cuz you're so deep in me beau   i can't get you outta my thoughts

beau
aww   ya got it all messed up   naw never
ya got it all wrong

geneviève
with all my love   geneviève

beau
yall got it all messed up

(lights fade on marshall and geneviève and office lights return to normal)

(crystal enters in black, takes a seat in 'interrogation room' beau is tightly wound returning from this memory)

beau
got anything to drink doc?

drummond
water

(interrogation lights up on crystal)

crystal
where is he now?

beau
anything else?

crystal
the place is so   quiet   now

drummond
what else would you like?

beau
coffee   coke   somethin

crystal
but
i'm not afraid anymore

drummond
what happened after they found the letter?
    mr. brown   we don't have much time left

beau
we surely have been gum flappin for a million years now

drummond
it might be good to take a break

i'll see what i can do about a coke
but when we get back beau   there are some things i
need you to be ready to tell me
why were you dishonorably discharged?
did it have to do with the prank?
who was the girl   the young vietnamese girl that
was crying   that grabbed you?

(beau is stony)

drummond
can you remember those questions beau? can you answer them when we get back?

crystal
he thinks i might—   but i'm...

beau
yeah doc

crystal
i'm stronger than that   i am

beau
i can tell you all about it

SEVEN

(light on crystal softens and expands to fill entire downstage space, which is now 'the apartment.' crystal crosses to downstage right. she is visibly waiting for something, though not impatiently. she is looking out of the window, sadly, but not overwhelmed with grief. a knock is heard offstage. crystal's head barely turns to acknowledge it. after a beat, marvin enters. crystal keeps vigil at the window)

crystal
am i a scarlet woman marvin?

marvin
whatchu mean baby?

crystal
havin two children wit a man i wouldn't marry

marvin
only scarlet as your heart is red i suppose

crystal
what brings you over this way?

marvin
wanted to see how you gettin on

crystal
first time you ever been to this place

marvin
can't honestly say that sugar   beau invite me
over for beers while you at work

(crystal smiles wanly)

crystal
you know where he is?

marvin
they got him downtown   say he's plum out
his mind   gonna see if he fit to stand trial

crystal
how long that take?

marvin
d.a. don't believe he crazy   think he just play acting
    they may give it about a week but the d.a. wanna
see him punished to the fullest extent of the law   and quick
    got a black doctor talkin to him so maybe he'll get
a break

crystal
got a black doctor talkin to him so he can't yell civil rights
    get one a your own to say you guilty
you know as good as me when it come to the law only color
is blue

marvin
maybe so

crystal
i dunno what to want marvin   all the pain he caused me
you'd think i'd wanna see him fry
but i know it's true about his head not bein right
    that make it okay to destroy everything?

i don't think so but killin another black man don't make things no better   i dunno what to want

marvin
you gotta want peace   that's all   that's all we can hope for now

(crystal turns to marvin)

crystal
oh i wanna hope for more than that marvin
i still wanna rich life
i wanna write poems n paint paintings n dance wit my eyes closed
i wanna be somethin stronger than i was before

marvin
you still young crystal   n beautiful as you ever been   n just as smart—

crystal
you think i'm beautiful?

marvin
of course i—

crystal
nobody said that to me any time i can remember
        knew i was pretty   hard to see sometimes but
knew i was once pretty n hoped it hadn't just disappeared
        guess it's hard to call another thing beautiful if
you feelin so ugly yourself

marvin
he knew how beautiful you are   he acted a fool
crystal but he does love you   that's the only reason—

crystal
you ever write a poem marvin?

(marvin struggles to hold back tears)

marvin
i'm sorry angel i know it was times i coulda saved you
        yall both needed savin
i wasn't brave enough to choose

crystal
ever love somebody?

marvin
whatchu gonna do now crystal?

crystal
was thinkin i'd go back to school   i wanna be a
teacher

marvin
you'd make a fine—

(crystal kisses marvin)

marvin
a-a-a fine teacher crystal

crystal
i think so

marvin
i've loved a few

crystal
(smiling) lovin just one nearly killed me   how you love a few?

marvin
man can only want for so long   some point he's got to have

crystal
n what you wanted you couldn't have?

marvin
baby doll   you kissed me a moment ago

crystal
i did

marvin
whatchu do that for?

crystal
you needed kissin

marvin
did i?

crystal
i needed to kiss

-

marvin
i try to be a good man crystal   i try   good man don't
love his brother's woman

crystal
marvin i think you talkin nonsense

marvin
naw crystal n you don't truly think that neither   it
tore me up   watchin my brother destroyin the
thing i loved   oh he loved you crystal but he
couldn't tell you what color brown you are i bet
    or know what your poems meant   mighta
made him feel like a big man to have a woman writing
poems about him but   beau ain't a real deep man you
know   i ain't sayin he dumb he just understand
things in his own way

you know that i coulda maybe saved you crystal
    maybe just one less broke rib   one less black eye
i was just too much a coward   afraid if i tried to stop him
it might come boilin out   come out my pores
    spill through my eyes   all the lovin i was doin
i was afraid yall could smell it on me   n if i thought for a
minute you'd love me back

but you ain't never loved nothin but beau   maybe
don't know how   n that's my brother   i couldn't
turn my back on him   not with the whole world
doin just that

crystal
i kissed you

marvin
you did

crystal
maybe i'm ready to learn

marvin
his smell still fresh on your sheets   i know you tryin to build new and move on fast as you can
     but i can't pretend he ain't still livin
specially when he's all alone without a friend in the world sides us

crystal
stay here with me marvin

marvin
angel i—

crystal
sleep in the other room   stay until this is over   i won't kiss you again i promise

marvin
i don't know where we be when this is over   but i'll take care of you long as you need me

crystal
let's be poetry when it's over marvin   let's be the sweetest poem ever written

(lights fade to dim, crystal exits, marvin exits opposite. lights go dimmer but not completely black)

SEVEN AND A HALF

(beau floats into the liminal space, indicated by lighting, between office and apartment, as though his ghost has come to see how marvin and crystal will get on without him. if there's a couch, perhaps he sits on it. he is ultra-lucid.)

(meanwhile, a tight spot lights drummond in the office. he speaks as though beau is there with him.)

drummond
...yeah   i have

beau
take all kindsa light

drummond
my mother collects prisms   a prism?   like glass
          glass cut to refract light

beau
light from the bedside lamp   the pilot on crystal stove

drummond
refract?   like bend   scatter

beau
light from the joint marvin pass when he see my pieces crumbling

drummond
is it violent you think beau?   what glass does to light?

beau
crystal take it all inside

drummond
how glass breaks light into its smallest parts
       or is it gentle   unfolding

beau
crystal take it all

(a knock is heard off-stage. sharp black on drummond. beau reacts. he's being called back to the reality of the office by the sound. crystal enters as if she has been woken up. beau and crystal pass each other, feel each other from their separate realities, but don't see each other. crystal starts for the door when marvin enters. he also has been awakened by this knock. beau recedes to the black of the office.)

EIGHT

(the knock is heard again, more persistent this time. marvin opens the door, geneviève enters)

crystal
aw hell naw marvin get this woman up outta my—

marvin
now angel just wait a minute

(to geneviève)

can i help you with something gal?

geneviève
i just had to see

crystal
marvin you better get this bitch up outta my house

geneviève
i just had to see what could've possibly taken him away from me

(crystal lunges at geneviève, but marvin stops her short and holds her. crystal strains against his hold.)

marvin
genie i think you'd better shuffle on it's late
      you been drinkin

crystal
filthy dirty—

marvin
crystal she ain't got no right up in your livin room but act like a lady still

geneviève
you didn't deserve him

crystal
you can have his crazy ass   if they don't send him to the chair first   cuz of what <u>you</u> done to him

marvin	**geneviève**
what <u>she</u> done?	if it weren't for you and those damn fuzzies you kept crankin out like a damn nigger factory –

(marvin releases crystal and she strikes geneviève. after they tussle for a few moments, marvin reluctantly intercedes to pull crystal off of geneviève and eventually gets her to calm down. while she perhaps stops trying to attack geneviève, she is incensed, chest heaving.)

crystal
fix   your   mouth
    tosayanotherwordaboutmychildren
and so help me god you will not leave this apartment still breathin

(geneviève is slumped against the wall, ragged from the beating)

geneviève
i loved him marvin   you know i did   will you tell the
girl?   he was the only thing
only man i've ever wrapped my arms around that didn't
treat me like a whore in the morning
he was hurting so bad   you were killing him   you and
these children   he could've been so many things
          did you even know he wanted to go back to school
so he could be a pilot?   that's what he had hoped for
joining the forces   before the accident happened
you couldnt've known   he never told you those things
          you'd rip his dreams to pieces before they even got
clean out of his mouth! i gave him the freedom to dream
          tell her marvin   i made him a king
          would you tell the girl?   i loved him the
way a woman should love a man   you don't know a
thing about that   i gave boy brown the
freedom to dream
you gave him headaches

crystal
marvin get this woman out of my house

geneviève
don't you put your hands on me

marvin
genie it's time for you to go

crystal
now

geneviève
his clothes   i just came to get his clothes   so when he gets out he won't have to come back here

marvin
i'm gonna walk her down crystal   i'll be right back

geneviève
i know they'll let him go soon   he's innocent
       i know you're the one that did it

crystal
marvin

geneviève
i'm gonna bake him a cake   vanilla frosting
welcome home in red letters

marvin
alright that's enough

(as marvin forces her out the door)

geneviève
but it's the best thing you ever done   we can be together now   it's the best thing you ever done

(crystal starts toward the door with a cold, steely fury. she stops herself just before exiting and takes a deep breath, trembling with rage. as she tries to calm herself down she is smashed with a tide of grief, collapsing with a long, plaintive wail. crystal is wracked by pain. marvin re-enters, wordlessly beginning to comfort her, holding her, stroking her hair.)

NINE

(marshall and geneviève enter in black, and sit on opposite sides in the 'interrogation room.' interrogation lights up on geneviève.)

geneviève
i know it for a fact   i'm telling you what i know   of course i'm sure   i went over there myself
i know what you boys think   think any white woman in love with a colored man can't be telling the truth
     didn't you listen to a word dr. king said
     about us all being equal and all that
ohyouknowwhatimean   i'm saying to you
     i know it for a fact   i went over there
to see for myself that's how   how long has beau been gone and already she's moved her pimp in
who knows what kinda operation they got runnin outta that apartment   i'm tellin you boys she's the one that did it   motive?   come on use your heads a little bit   the motive is now she can whore around full time   already she moves the pimp in
     isn't that proof enough?
besides you know how these colored women can be
     not a care in the world except for money and
what's between a man's legs   i know it for a fact boys
     so you might as well just let him go   didn't
you hear a word dr. king said about peace and
understanding   so why don't you let the poor boy
go already   you got the truth now anyway

(simultaneous fade on geneviève and lights up on marshall. geneviève exits)

TEN

marshall
i had taken up with one of the local girls   prettiest tiny
little thing   of course there was a language barrier
but not much talking was necessary if you know what i
mean

you boys don't know what it was like out there   over
here protesting picketing spitting at our men
  i don't really like telling all of this because i know what
you'll think   but   a man's life
hangs in the balance i suppose

beau willie brown would have been a fine soldier
  good instincts you know?

come on boys stay with me   i <u>know</u> you know what i
mean about <u>instincts</u>
  yes YES   he was loony   on the record if you
must but he had amazing instincts   knew just where
the gooks were hiding   could smell the difference in the
air if someone was crouching in the vines   he had a
knack for killing   not because he was
strong   or fast   or <u>smart</u> lord knows   it
was his instincts

now for the record   most of this i did not see myself
i only saw what i saw   the rest was told to me by
isaacs and brooks   good kids   rotten soldiers
  two boys in beau's same platoon
beau had gotten really plastered   a letter came from
home they tell me
        bad news i guess

    i couldn't tell you exactly   but beau sure was in a slump
and i guess tried to drink his way out of it

well i was hoping for a little r&r with my girl that night
i went over to her place and she wasn't there
      her two kids were missing too which struck me as
very odd   i started walking toward the
hooch to ask some of the boys is they'd seen her
everyone knew she was my girl
  she was the only pretty thing in the village   well as
i'm walking brooks comes running toward me
                says i better come quick
something i might want to see

my girl's kneeling in the mud
                beau's got her by the hair with this awful
                look on his face
                        a few feet away private
                        isaacs is untying her two
                        young ones

said beau threatened to shoot them if they came any closer

when beau sees me   this wild look comes in his eyes
like some sort of trapped animal
and he hits her   knocks her clean away from him and she
hits her head on one of the trash cans

what really got me was the children   he made
them watch   the youngest   the little boy
he was screaming crying   red and little round cheeks
glossed with tears   but the older child
the girl   she was   expressionless   like a
statue   looking past us all

like she was never coming back

-

i couldn't fight a war with that kind of filth in my
battalion   and i needed him
he would've made a fine soldier   i knew he wasn't
quite right in the head   i just recommended he
be sent home   but believe you me he should've
spent some time in the stockade   so this
doesn't surprise me   not a bit

it's about time someone lock him up   i don't give a
damn if the cell is padded or not

(quick black on marshall)

ELEVEN

(lights up quick on the office. beau is telling his side of the story, the scene rising in the middle of this conversation)

drummond
how did you know she was marshall's girl?

beau
at first i didn't   when he came up   i saw his face   i looked down at hers again then

drummond
you slapped her

beau
naw i   doc   i ain't never had to take nothin from a woman   the way sarge looked at me

drummond
alright   let's take this one step at a time   you were relieving yourself near the trash behind the tavern before you could zip your pants someone grabbed you from behind

beau
doc what's this got to do with anything at all   what's this got to do with anything   this ain't meant for nobody to hear   what's this got to do with anything at all   some things in a man's life don't need repeatin

drummond
please beau   i need to understand

\-

beau
the children   a girl about four n the boy   two
maybe isaacs tied em up   tied together wit they
little wrists behind they backs turnin purple from the knots
     n a rope around they necks he act like he'd strangle
em wit if she ain't do what they say

drummond
go on

(crystal appears sometime throughout this monologue with movement interpretations of beau's narration, however at this point, she is no longer relegated to any particular region of the stage, moves freely through the office, the apartment, the interrogation room, etc.)

beau
i'd drank bout enough to fill a bathtub   when she grabbed
me i don't know what i thought   i was scared but
     im a man doc   it'd been a long time

\-

i could tell she been cryin before i even turnt around
though   n i done some devilish shit in my life doc
     but takin nothin from no woman ain't one of em
       no real man could   no real
man would want to   so for a moment i relaxed into her
hands   but a moment later i knew i didn't want
nothin she was givin   couldn't stop her though
    her eyes beggin for her childrens life

for me to jus let her so the boys would let em go n not hurt
em none too bad   when she started i grabbed her by
the hair   not rough or nothin   just tried to get
her off me   i didn't want it n she didn't want
to do it so why we was in this silly fix was beatin the hell
outta me   but she got crazy   making
this terrible screamin cryin sound   diggin her nails
into my thighs like the talons of some mama bird ready to
whup ass for its young   then i follow her eyes to the
children
isaacs pull the rope up
the boys brown feet just barely can catch the ground now
         i wanna push away again n the rope yanks higher
       she grab me tighter   his lil brown toes scrapin
to get hold of the mud
she pull me harder   coulda been any brown boy in a
mississippi sycamore   cept we a hundred million miles
from mississipi n ain't no trees   jus a fucked up
charlie holdin a saturday night thrill at the end of some
rope

n i can't move   can't breathe   like it's me swingin from
the end of his rope

she jus go on doin what she need to do n i'm froze up cuz i
catch the eyes of the older one
i can't   breathe   she lookin at me dead up
       her eyes are two glass beads
or the black stones i seen in this ring crystal wear
         the lil boy is throwin a fit to wake heaven but the
girl is   barely movin   barely   breathin   her eyes
lock me

i know i seen them eyes before

i'm standin over crystal   she's twitchin   i got
kwame beau jr over my head in the high chair
naomi standin against the refrigerator   still as a tree
      kwame hollerin so loud i think his head might pop
clear off   but naomi   my baby girl   is
lookin at me   like she her mama spirit step up
out her body to watch what i'm doin to it   i stand
there   locked

next thing i know i'm walkin   the sun is makin my
fingers hot   the inbetween skin is sticky n red
      them eyes   i can't get outta my head   i
had never noticed em before but they been there every
time   all the fights me n crystal had   since
before kwame was born even   naomi was there
most times   she must've been standin by the wall givin
her daddy that same look every time   n i didn't see em
till just then

that's when the notion hit me   i been somethin awful to
them gals   n little kwame beau jr too   wasn't a
damn thing i could do to make bread for my family when i
got back   seems like everything i tried   all i got
was turned backs   but crystal
      my piece of rainbow   she was still good
for makin something beautiful outta a whole heap a ugly
      she took beau willie brown n made two babies god
hisself must've made the mold for

time to be a man   marry that woman   make us a
family

drummond
but she didn't want to get married

beau
n the little girl tied up to her brother is watchin me with a
handful of her mama's hair   her eyes are black glass
       my daughters eyes when she look at her daddy n
see a monster   n i want to go untie the little girl n the
baby boy   hug em n tell em it's gonna be alright
       i don't wanna hurt yo mama none

i jus wanna marry her   n be nice   n give her thangs

kwame is screamin but naomi's so quiet   reachin
       n a little scared   that little girls eyes
       flash in her face

*(lights up on crystal downstage – an excerpt from 'for colored
girls…'during the following sequence, 'the office' disappears
and only crystal and beau, in separate lights, are visible)*

crystal
he kicked the screen outta the window/ & held the kids offa
the sill

beau
that little girls eyes flash in her face   n i can't breathe
       like all the air in the room bein
sucked into naomi's little black eyes

crystal
i stood by beau in the window

beau
like all the color in the room bein sucked into the black a
her eyes

96

crystal
with naomi reachin for me/ and kwame screamin mommy
mommy from the fifth story

beau
naomi   is so quiet   her eyes sayin
everything her mama been tellin me since i got back

crystal   **beau**
i stood by beau in the window   n i can't breathe

beau
her eyes are sayin everything   you couldn't save
that little black eyed girl n her brother
          you couldn't even save yourself

crystal
with naomi reachin for me

beau
her eyes are sayin everything   you can't save me
either daddy

crystal
and kwame screamin mommy mommy from the fifth story

beau
all the air in the room bein sucked in to naomi's little black
eyes   tell me it's gonna be alright daddy
n i can't breathe   i can't say anything
tell me tell me tell me tell me it's gonna be alright daddy
          but i cd only whisper

crystal
i stood by beau in the window

beau
i just   let go   just let them   go

(lights fade on crystal, she disappears. lights back up on drummond, 'the office' reappears)

beau
(realizing)
doc? doc?   aww nawwwww doc

(beau is doubled over with grief, struck with a blow to the belly – the knowledge that he has killed his own two children. beau screams. he is writhing on the office floor, screaming adlibs of "naw doc, naw…" drummond goes to him, and partially hugging him, partially restraining him, wraps his arms around beau's torso as he continues to wail. lights fade to black)

EPILOGUE

(lights up on the office. drummond is there alone. some time has passed. he sits scribbling on a yellow legal pad. he stands slowly and paces his office, considering heavily its many artifacts, his framed degree hanging on the back wall, etc. he sits down, now at his desk and begins deliberately typing away at his typewriter. after several moments, he considers what he has written. his face contorts as though he is about to lose composure, but without a beat, he regroups himself and becomes stoic. he takes the page he has written out of the typewriter, make a note or two on it, and begins reading from it.)

This is the story you will never hear. No manicured news anchor will bring this to your living room with red lips twisted in well-rehearsed concern. This is the story that sticks in the throat. This is the question that pleads silently in the throat unable to draw a breath. You will not see this story smeared in a whimsical sidebar of some evening post left in the seat next to you on the bus. Your local radio personality will not ask you to call in and give your opinion about it. This is the story that bleeds in the dark. This is the story that creaks softly in the purple breeze of Mississippi midnights.

(beau enters. he is a ghost. like crystal in the previous scene, he is no longer confined to the reality of a particular space and moves freely through all places and times. movement interpretation: he dies in the moment of realization over and over and over. he is destroyed only to be destroyed again, with no relief. as drummond continues, the lights begin to fade on the office, so that only he and beau are fully lit. then the light on him fades until only beau is lit. as this lighting shifts,

moments of rebirth begin to appear in beau's dance. he continues to die, but now, is reborn again. and dies, and is reborn, and dies....)

I am no one special to tell this story, and truthfully, I didn't want to do it. But another man's bad dreams kick me awake at night. And I want to sleep again.

So this is the dirge painted on the open mouths of brown mothers. This is the song that bursts strident from the lungs of Black men when no one is around to hear. The warrior chant drumming bravely through the vines.

This is the story you will not hear and you have heard it a million times. It ripples across the flesh of our myths. It is the ghost sipping coffee at your kitchen table.

(beau stops dying altogether. he is reborn and reborn and reborn. he flies. and is reborn)

Perhaps every man must wade in the mire of his mind, in the quiet before dawn, without a flame or the hint of morning to light the way. Perhaps every man must claw through the mud of his nightmares, hoping an angel will be there to bless him at daybreak. I am allowed to witness this.

All such journeys are not created equal. There is rarely someone there to hear the mumbles of your night terrors, whispers curdling around your sleeping lips barely audible above your heartbeat. I have been allowed to listen. This is the story murmured between dark dreams, for those that never wake.

(lights begin to fade on beau as he continues to be reborn. he is awakened. before the lights fade to black, he freezes in what would be triumph, but is only relief. his eyes are open. he is awake.)

blackout

(lights begin to fade on beau as he continues to be reborn. he is awakened. before the lights fade to black, he freezes in what would be triumph, but is only relief. his eyes are open. he is awake.)

blackout